NATURAL DISASTERS

A Volcano Erupts

Susan Bullen

Wayland

Natural Disasters

A Storm Rages
A Volcano Erupts
Flood Damage
The Power of
Earthquakes

Editor: Deb Elliott
Designer: Malcolm Walker
Cover pictures: background – The view across the ancient Tengger volcano crater in East Java, Indonesia. left – Lava flows from the Nyiragongo volcano in Zaire. middle – The Stromboli volcano erupting. right – The eruption in 1959 of Kilauea-Iki. A fountain of lava can be seen above the trees along the rim of the crater.

Text is based on *Volcano* in *The Violent Earth* series published in 1992

First published in 1994 by
Wayland (Publishers) Ltd
61, Western Road, Hove
East Sussex, BN3 1JD, England

British Library Cataloguing in Publication Data
Bullen, Susan
  Volcano Erupts. - (Natural Disasters Series)
  I. Title II. Series
  551.2

ISBN 0 7502 1186 5

Typeset by Kudos
Printed and bound by
  Rotolito Lambarda s.p.a.

Contents

◀   *This red-hot volcano looks more like a firework display!*

A mountain on fire!

Look at this cone-shaped mountain. We call it a volcano. This volcano is in the USA. It is called Mount St Helens.

Can you see the snow on Mount St Helens? ▶

▼ *A newspaper story about a volcano.*

Big New Rain of Ash

VOLCANO BLOWS AGAIN

San Francisco Chronicle

The Largest Daily Circulation in Northern California

116th Year No. 128 ★★★★ FRIDAY, JUNE 13, 1980 777-1111 20 CENTS

Tortured Terrain	Clouds of Ash Fall Over Cities

Some volcanoes blow up. This happened to Mount St Helens in March 1980. Clouds of black smoke came out of the top. It looked like the volcano was on fire.

'The cloud was like a wall about 3 miles across', said a man talking about Mount St Helens.

◀ *The smoke from Mount St Helens went high into the sky.*

ruined forest

ash cloud

mud flows

the area that was damaged

Mount St Helens

NORTH
AMERICA

Mount St Helens

0   10km

◀ *The main areas of devastation caused by the eruption of Mount St Helens.*

All these trees were burnt down when the volcano exploded. ▶

'Huge old fir trees were flattened like a million wooden matches.'

Inside Mount St Helens it was hot enough to melt rock. Red-hot lava flowed out of the volcano, like rivers of fire. The volcano eruption killed fifty-seven people and two million forest animals.

◀ *This is Mount St Helens today. Its top was blown off in 1980.*

How do volcanoes happen?

Volcanoes begin deep inside the Earth. Right inside the liquid core it is hotter than fire. Outside the core is the mantle. This is more solid, but still very hot. Around the mantle is the Earth's crust, with land and sea on top.

Looking inside the Earth

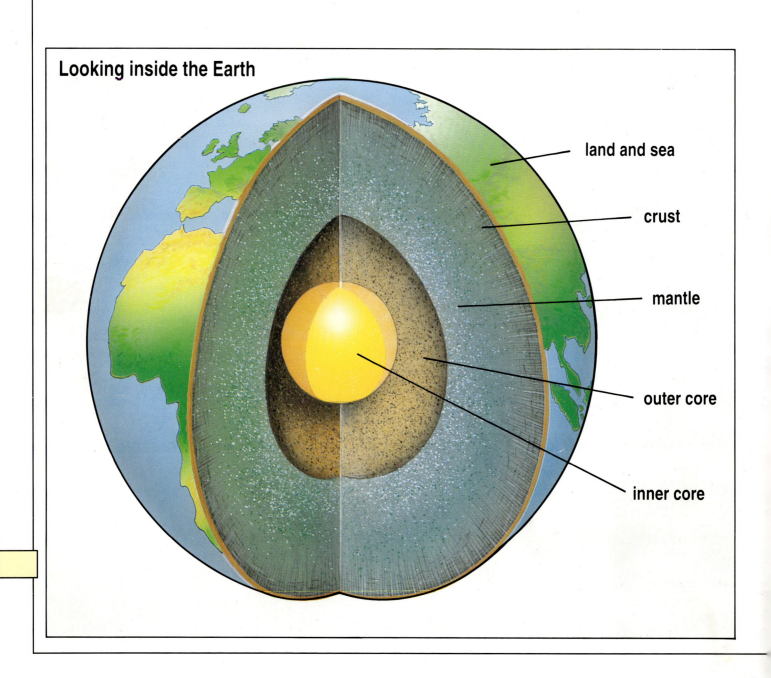

land and sea

crust

mantle

outer core

inner core

When a volcano erupts, it gets rid of heat from deep inside the Earth. In the mantle and crust, rocks melt down into magma. The magma rises up inside the volcano and bursts out as lava and smoke.

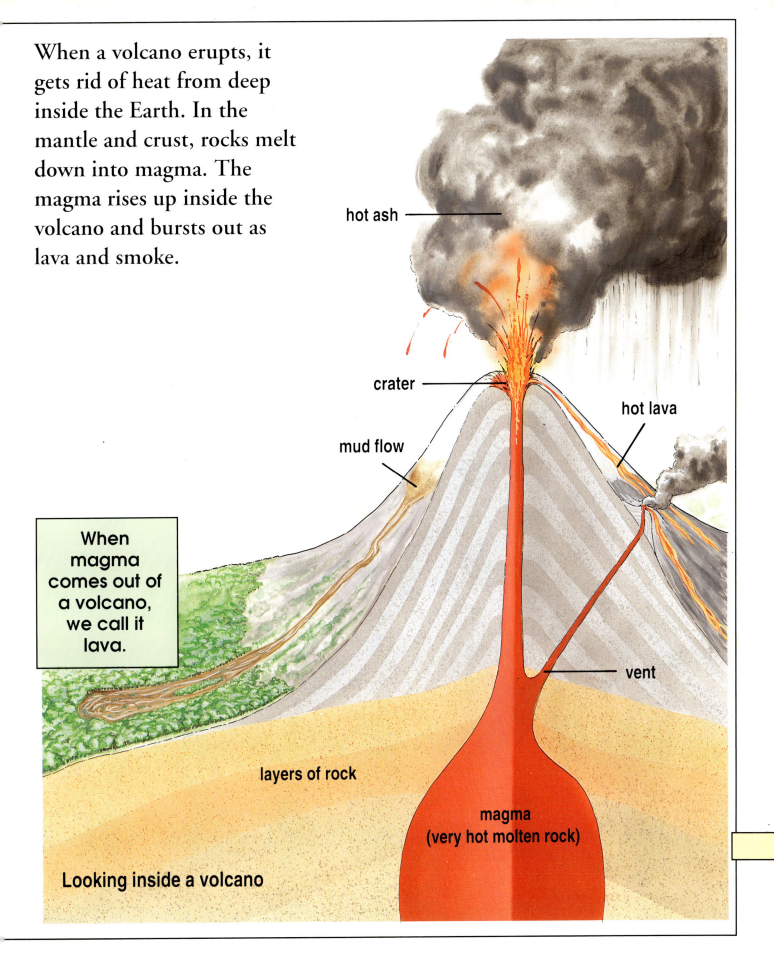

hot ash

crater

hot lava

mud flow

When magma comes out of a volcano, we call it lava.

vent

layers of rock

magma
(very hot molten rock)

Looking inside a volcano

Where volcanoes happen

Below the land and sea is the Earth's crust. It is made of huge segments of rock called plates. Sometimes magma is squeezed up between two plates. Then a volcano forms.

Some volcanoes are not found near plate edges. They are made when magma comes up through hot spots where the crust is thinner.

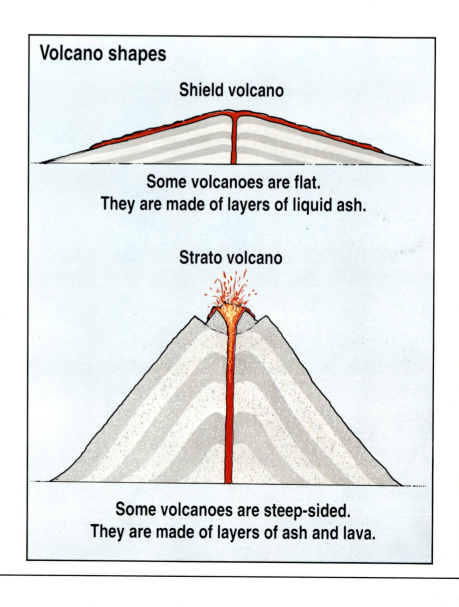

Volcano shapes

Shield volcano

Some volcanoes are flat.
They are made of layers of liquid ash.

Strato volcano

Some volcanoes are steep-sided.
They are made of layers of ash and lava.

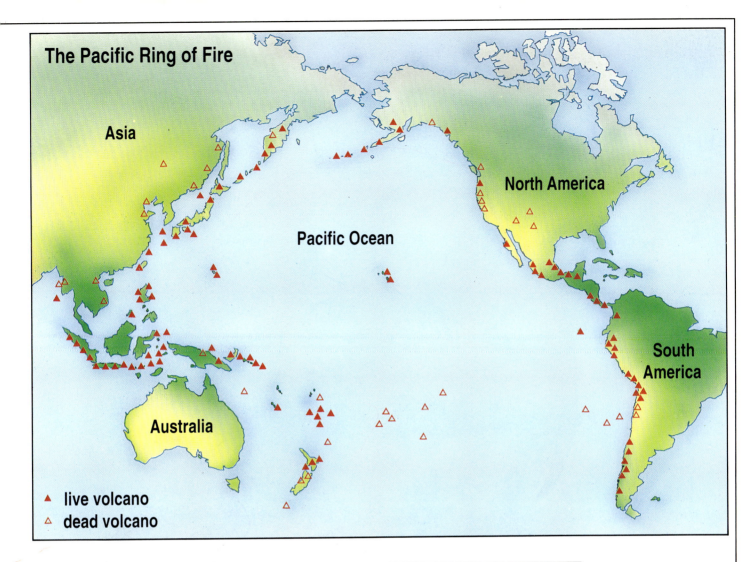

The Pacific Ring of Fire

Asia

North America

Pacific Ocean

South America

Australia

▲ live volcano
△ dead volcano

▲ *Many volcanoes occur at plate edges around the Pacific Ocean.*

◀ *Look at the red-hot lava from this angry volcano!*

11

Volcano islands

Some volcanoes make islands in the sea. Here you can see a new volcanic island called Surtsey. It came out of the sea near Iceland in November 1963.

▼   *Steam and lava come from Surtsey as it is born.*

How Surtsey was born

1. Huge bubbles came up into the sea. Below them, hot magma was rising from the sea-bed.

2. Next, hot lava flowed out. It mixed with cold sea water.

3. Then the lava cooled and became hard. It made a new rocky island.

Surtsey is 170 m high and about 1 km across. Today some plants, birds and insects live on the island.

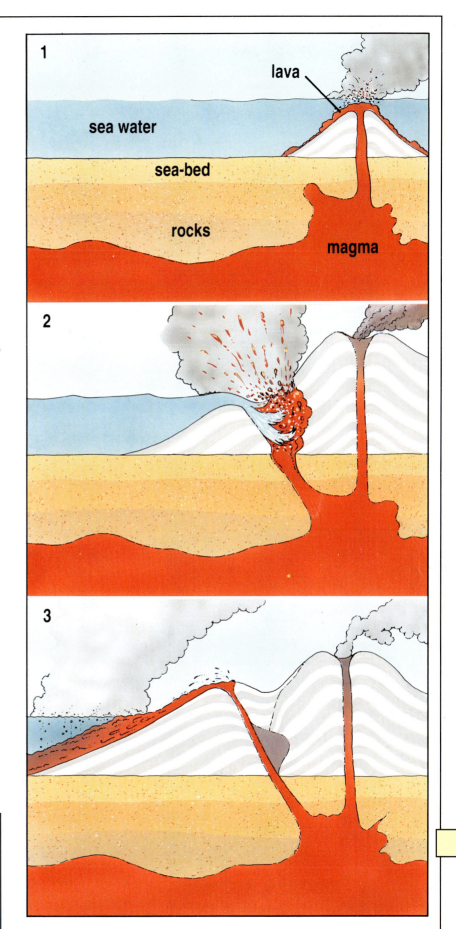

13

Volcanoes in the past

In August 1883 a huge explosion happened in Krakatoa in Indonesia. This volcanic island blew itself in half. Then huge waves followed and they swept away 36,000 people on other islands.

▼ *A picture of Krakatoa exploding in 1883.*

How Krakatoa has changed

1. Before 1883 Krakatoa looked like this.

When Krakatoa exploded, it sent shock waves around the world. Smoke and dust from the burning volcano made bright sunsets in the sky.

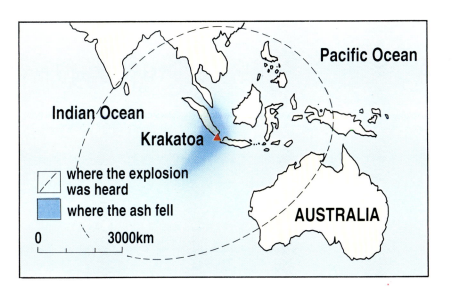

2. After 1883 most of the island was blown away. It left a big crater in the sea-bed.

3. After 1927 Krakatoa looked different again. A new island had grown in the crater.

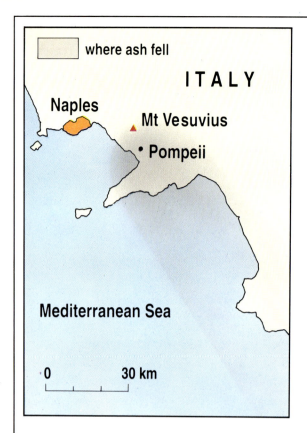

Date	Place	What happened
1450 BC	Santorini, Greece	Destroyed
79 AD	Mt Vesuvius, Italy	20,000 dead
1586	Kelud, Java	10,000 dead
1669	Mt Etna, Sicily	20,000 dead
1792	Mt Unzen, Japan	15,000 dead
1815	Tambora, Indonesia	90,000 dead
1883	Krakatoa, Indonesia	36,000 dead

A famous volcano disaster happened in Italy, a long time ago. In AD 79 Mount Vesuvius exploded and hot ash buried the city of Pompeii. It killed 20,000 people.

Plaster casts of victims of Pompeii. ▶

After Mount Vesuvius exploded, Pompeii lay buried for many centuries. In 1861 people dug out the ancient city. They found streets of houses with cooking pots and tools inside.

▼ *These are the ruins of Pompeii.*

Volcanoes in modern times

Some big volcanoes have erupted this century, too. In 1902 Mont Pelée blew up on the Caribbean island of Martinique. Poisonous fumes and hot ash poured out and destroyed the nearby town of St Pierre. About 28,000 people were killed.

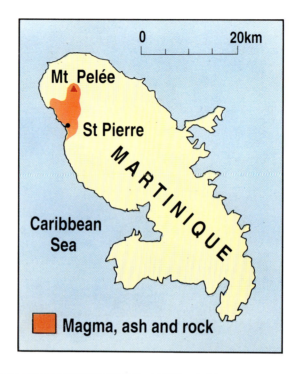

◄ *A map of Martinique and its volcano Mont Pelée.*

All this smoke came from Mont Pelée in 1902. ▶

On 13 November 1985, the volcano Nevada del Ruiz exploded in the Andes Mountains of Colombia. Then a huge mud flow rushed down the mountainside and killed 25,000 people in the town of Almero below.

Rescue workers look for survivors in Almero. ▶

▼ *Colombia is a country in South America.*

Volcanoes in the twentieth century		
Date	Place	Deaths
1902	Mont Pelée, Martinique	34,000
1906	Mt Vesuvius, Italy	700
1951	Mt Lamington, Papua New Guinea	3,000
1980	Mt St Helens, USA	57
1985	Nevada del Ruiz, Colombia	25,000
1991	Mt Unzen, Japan	41
1991	Mt Pinatubo, Philippines	400

In Japan there is a volcano called Mount Unzen. In 1792 it erupted and killed 15,000 people. On 3 June 1991, Mount Unzen blew up again. Floods of lava ruined many homes but luckily most people escaped in time.

A survivor runs from the smoke and heat of Mount Unzen. ▶

▼ *Can you see two volcanoes on this map?*

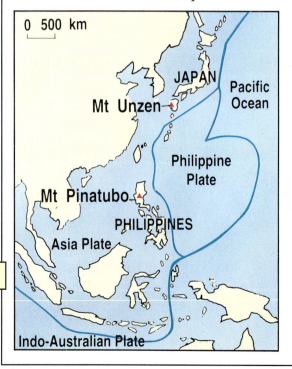

Another big volcano erupted in June 1991. Mount Pinatubo in the Philippines had been sleeping for 600 years. Then in 1991 it suddenly roared loudly and a huge cloud of ash rose into the sky. The ash spread over Singapore, Malaysia and Vietnam.

▼ *Mount Pinatubo covered this street in deep ash.*

When do volcanoes happen?

Some volcanoes give warning signs before they explode. Smoke comes from the top and nearby ground trembles. But some volcanoes stay quiet and blow up very suddenly. Sometimes hot water is pumped to the surface by digging wells.

▼ *Lava flows often come from Mount Etna in Sicily.*

Some people study volcanoes, watching for danger signs. They also measure movements in the ground. Then they try to work out where the next explosion will be.

▼ *This man is testing gas from a volcano. Look at his heat-proof suit.*

Helpful or harmful?

Volcanoes are dangerous but they can be useful, too. The hot magma below a volcano can heat up underground water. It comes out of the ground as a hot spring.

▼ *Hot magma warms up water all over the world.*

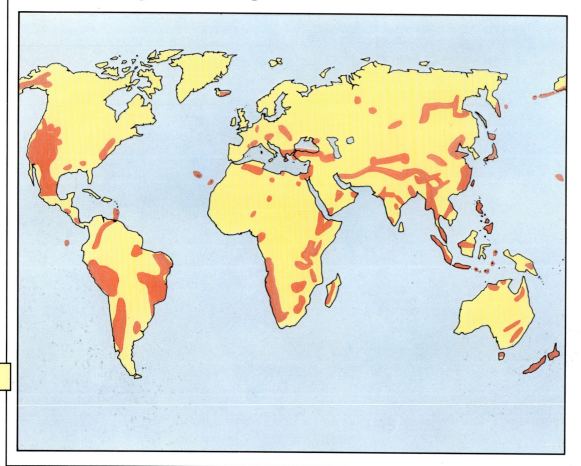

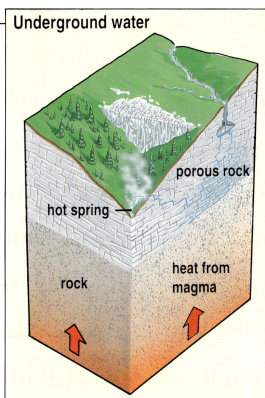

Underground water

porous rock

hot spring

rock

heat from magma

In Japan people bathe in hot springs. In some countries people use the hot water for cooking.

▲ *Hot rocks heat up underground water from underneath.*

Some hot springs are like big fountains. We call them geysers. ▶

Volcanoes also help farmers because lava makes a rich soil. It contains many minerals that help plants to grow. People grow crops in lava in Indonesia, India, Italy and the Canary Islands.

▼ *In Indonesia people use lava as a fertilizer for crops.*

So, volcanoes sometimes help people. But when they blow up, we remember how dangerous they are. What do you think about volcanoes?

▼ *This angry volcano is Mount Ngauruhoe in New Zealand.*

Project: Make a model volcano

What to do:

1 Ask an adult to help you. First, look again at the photos of volcanoes in this book.

2 Shape the volcano from the chicken wire. Make a crater in the top. Put the plastic tub inside.

3 Mix up the paste. Cut the newspaper into pieces. Soak it in the paste for 5 minutes.

4 Cover the wire volcano shape with three layers of newspapers.

5 When it is dry, paint on the landscape. You can add model trees and houses.

You need:
stiff card (50 cm x 50 cm)
chicken wire mesh (75 cm x 75 cm)
small plastic tub
wallpaper paste
old newspapers
waterproof paints
bright red plasticine or tissue paper

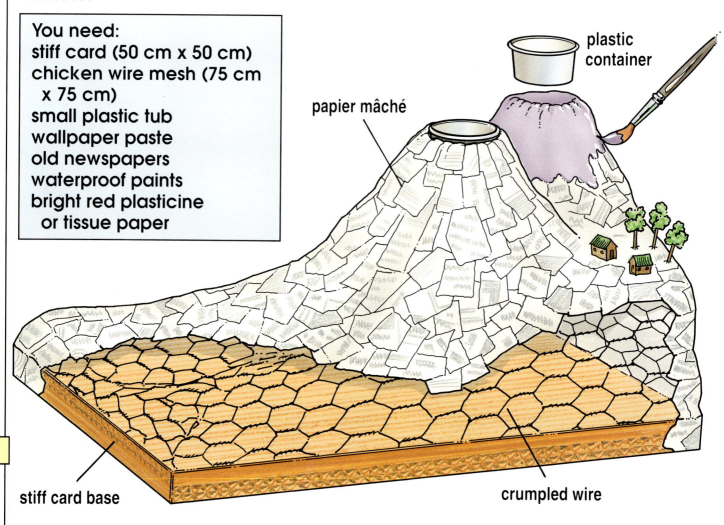

plastic container

papier mâché

stiff card base

crumpled wire

Now you can add the lava.

6 Put lots of plasticine or crumpled tissue paper inside the crater.
Then make it flow down the slope of the volcano.

Can you think of a name
for your angry volcano?

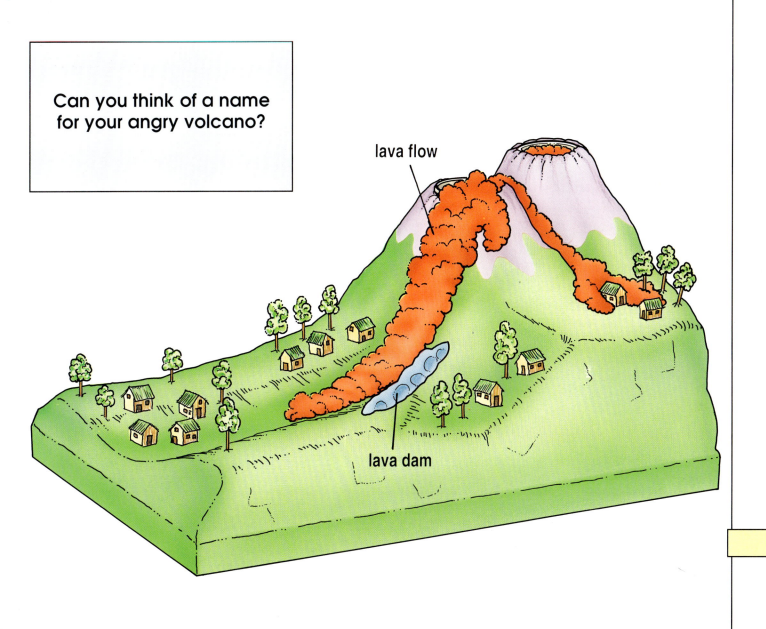

lava flow

lava dam

Glossary

ancient From long ago.

ash The dry, dusty remains from a fire.

core The centre of the Earth.

eruption The name for a volcanic explosion.

exploded Blew up.

fertilizer Something put on to crops to make them grow better.

lava Red-hot, molten rock that flows out of a volcano.

magma The very hot mixture of solid and molten rock that forms deep inside the Earth.

mantle The part of the Earth between the inner core and outer crust.

molten Melted into a liquid.

rescue workers People who save other people from danger.

steam A mist of tiny water droplets in the air.

volcanic island A volcano that makes an island in the sea.

Books to read

Natural Disasters by Tim Wood
    (Wayland, 1993)
The Eruption of Krakatoa by Rupert
    Matthews (Wayland, 1988)

Picture acknowledgements
The photographs in this book were supplied by
The Associated Press Ltd 20; Associated
Press/Topham 5, 14; Bruce Coleman Ltd cover
(background Gerald Cubitt), (left, Dieter and
Mary Plage), (middle, Fritz Prenzel), (right,
Werner Stoy),16 (bottom, Melinda Berge), 26
(Fritz Prenzel); John Frost's Historical Newspapers
4 (left); Geoscience Features Picture Library 18 (A.
Lacroix), 22, 23 (Basil Booth); Frank Lane Picture
Agency 4 (right, USDA Forest Service), 7 (J.W.
Hughes, USDA); Oxford Scientific Films 12
(Hjalmar R. Bardarson), 25 (Michael Fogden);
Photri imprint/contents page, 6-7, 11; Frank
Spooner Pictures 19, 21; Tony Stone Worldwide
27; Werner Forman Archive 16-17. All artwork is
by Nick Hawken.

Index